The Expedition
of Burke and Wills
& the Search to Find Them

by
Burke, Wills, King, and Walker

Contents

Part One:
Expedition of Burke and Wills

by
Burke, Wills, and King

Introduction

The purpose of the Burke and Wills expedition, which set out from Melbourne in 1860, was to cross the continent [of Australia] from south to north. By making a dash from his depot on Cooper's Creek, Burke succeeded in reaching the mouth of the Flinders River, which flows into the Gulf of Carpentaria. But through a series of mishaps, tragedy marked the end of the expedition. The two leaders perished from thirst and starvation on the Barcoo, and one of the men who had accompanied them, Gray, also died, of exhaustion. The fourth of the party, King, saved his life through the kindness of a native tribe with which he took refuge. The three following narratives [in this section] consist of Burke's last despatch, which was found amongst the papers found at Cooper's Creek; of King's narrative and of Wills's account of the dash from Cooper's Creek to the Gulf. The two first-mentioned documents are contained in the pamphlet on *The Burke and Wills Exploring Expedition*, published at Melbourne, 1861; the third is from Wills's journal, published in the volume entitled *A Successful Exploration through the Interior of Australia*, compiled from Wills's papers by his father, and published at London, 1863.

Burke's Last Despatch

The following is the last despatch written by Mr. Burke. It was found amongst the papers deposited on Cooper's Creek:

Depot 2, Cooper's Creek Camp 65.—

The return party from Carpentaria, consisting of myself, Wills, and King (Gray dead), arrived here last night and found that the depot party had only started on the same day. We proceed on, to-morrow, slowly down the creek towards Adelaide by Mount Hopeless, and shall endeavour to follow Gregory's track; but we are very weak. The two camels are done up, and we shall not be able to travel faster than four or five miles a day. Gray died on the road, from exhaustion and fatigue. We have all suffered much from hunger. The provisions left here will, I think, restore our strength. We have discovered a practicable route to Carpentaria, the chief position of which lies in the 140 degrees of East longitude. There is some good country between this and the Stony Desert. From thence to the tropics the land is dry and stony. Between the Carpentaria a considerable portion is rangy, but well watered and richly grassed. We reached the shores of Carpentaria on the 11th of February, 1861. Greatly disappointed at finding the party here gone.

(Signed) ROBERT O'HARA BURKE, Leader, April 22, 1861.

P.S. The camels cannot travel, and we cannot walk, or we should follow the other party. We shall move very slowly down the creek.

King's Narrative

Mr. Burke, Mr. Wills, and I, reached the depot at Cooper's Creek, on April 2 1st, about half-past seven in the evening, with two camels; all that remained of the six Mr. Burke took with him. All the provisions we then had consisted of one-and-a-half pound of dried meat. We found the party had gone the same day; and looking about for any mark they might have left, found the tree with 'DIG, Ap. 21.' Mr. Wills said the party had left for the Darling. We dug and found the plant of stores. Mr. Burke took the papers out of the bottle, and then asked each of us whether we were able to proceed up the creek in pursuit of the party; we said not, and he then said that he thought it his duty to ask us, but that he himself was unable to do so, but that he had decided upon trying to make Mount Hopeless, as he had been assured by the Committee in Melbourne, that there was a cattle station within 150 miles of Cooper's Creek. Mr. Wills was not inclined to follow this plan, and wished to go down our old track; but at last gave in to Mr. Burke's wishes. I also wished to go down by our old track. We remained four or five days to recruit, making preparations to go down the creek by stages of four or five miles a day, and Mr. Burke placed a paper in the plant stating what were our plans. Travelling down the creek, we got some fish from the natives; and some distance down, one of the camels (Landa) got bogged, and although we remained there that day and part of the next, trying to dig him out, we found our strength insufficient to do so. The evening of the second day we shot him as he lay, and having cut off as much meat as we could, we lived on it while we stayed to dry the remainder. Throwing all the least necessary things away, we made one load for the remaining camel (Rajah), and each of us carried a swag of about twenty-five pounds. We were then tracing down the branches of the creek running south, and found that they ran out into earthy plains. We had understood that the creek along Gregory's track was continuous; and finding that all these creeks ran out into plains, Mr. Burke returned, our camel being completely knocked up. We then intended to give the camel a spell for a few days, and to make a new attempt to push on forty or fifty miles to the south, in the hope of striking the creek. During the time that the camel was being rested, Mr. Burke and Mr. Wills went in search of the natives, to endeavour to find out how the nardoo grew. Having found their camp, they obtained as much nardoo cake and fish as they could eat, but could not explain that they wished to be shown how to find the seed themselves: they returned on the third day bringing some fish and nardoo cake with them. On the following day the camel Rajah seemed very ill, and I told Mr. Burke I thought he could not linger out more than four days, and as on the same evening the poor brute was on the point of dying, Mr. Burke ordered him to be shot; I did so, and we cut him up with two broken knives and a lancet: we cured the meat and planted it, and Mr. Burke then made another attempt to find the nardoo, taking me with him: we went down the creek expecting to find the natives at the camp where they had been last seen, but found that they had left; and not knowing whether they had gone up or down the creek, we slept in their gunyahs that night, and on the following morning returned to Mr. Wills. The next day, Mr. Burke and I started up the creek, but could see nothing of them, and were three days away, when we returned and remained three days in our camp with Mr. Wills. We then made a plant of all the articles we could not carry with us, leaving five pounds of rice and a quantity of meat, and then followed up the creek to where there were some good native huts. We remained at that place a few days; and finding that our provisions were beginning to run short, Mr. Burke said, that we ought to do something, and that if we did not find the nardoo, we should starve, and that he intended to save a little dried meat and rice to carry us to Mount Hopeless. The three of us then came to the conclusion that it would be better to make a second attempt to reach Mount Hopeless, as we were then as strong as we were likely to be, our daily allowance being then reduced. Mr. Burke asked each of us whether we were willing to make another attempt to reach the South Australian settlements, and we decided on going; we took with us what remained of the provisions we had planted two-and-a-half pounds of oatmeal, a small quantity of flour, and the dried meat: this, with powder and shot, and other small articles, made up our swags to thirty pounds each, and Mr. Burke carried one billy of water; and I another. We had not gone far before we came on a flat, where I saw a plant growing which I took to be clover, and on looking closer saw the seed, and called out that I had found the nardoo; they were very glad when I found it. We travelled three days, and struck a watercourse coming south from Cooper's Creek; we traced this as it branched out and re-formed in the plains, until we at last lost it in flat country; sandhills were in front of us, for which we made, and travelled all day but found no water. We were all greatly fatigued, as our rations now consisted of only one small Johnny cake and three sticks of dried meat daily. We camped that evening about four o'clock, intending to push next day until two o'clock P.M., and then, should we not find water, to return. We travelled and found no water, and the three of us sat down and rested for one hour, and then turned back. We all felt satisfied that had there been a few days' rain we could have got through: we were then, according to Mr. Wills's calculation, forty-five miles from the creek. We travelled, on the day we turned back, very late, and the following evening reached the nearest water at the creek. We gathered some nardoo and boiled the seeds, as we were unable to pound them. The following day we reached the main creek; and knowing where there was a fine waterhole and native gunyahs, we went there intending to save what remained of our flour and dried meat for the purpose of making another attempt to reach Mount Hopeless. On the following day Mr. Wills and I went out to gather nardoo, of which we obtained a supply sufficient for three days, and finding a pounding stone at the gunyahs, Mr. Burke and I pounded the seed, which was such slow work that we were compelled to use half flour and half nardoo. Mr. Burke and Mr. Wills then went down the creek for the remainder of the dried meat which we had planted; and we had now all our things with us, gathering nardoo and living the best way we could. Mr. Burke requested Mr. Wills to go up the creek as far as the depot, and to place a note in the plant there, stating that we were then living on the creek, the former note having stated that we were on our road to South Australia. He also was to bury there the field-books of the journey to the Gulf. Before starting he got three pounds of flour and four pounds of pounded nardoo, and about a pound of meat, as he expected to be absent about eight days. During his absence I gathered nardoo and pounded it, as Mr. 'Burke wished to lay in a supply in case of rain.

A few days after Mr. Wills left, some natives came down the creek to fish at some waterholes near our camp. They were very civil to us at first and offered us some fish. On the second day they came again to fish, and Mr. Burke took down two bags, which they filled for him. On the third day they gave us one bag of fish, and afterwards all came to our camp. We used to keep our ammunition and other articles in one gunyah, and all three of us lived together in another. One of the natives took an oilcloth out of this gunyah, and Mr. Burke seeing him run away with it followed him with his revolver and fired over his head, and upon this the native dropt the oilcloth; while he was away, the other blacks invited me away to a waterhole to eat fish, but I declined to do so as Mr. Burke was absent, and a number of natives were about who would have taken all our things. When I refused, one took his boomerang and laid it over my shoulder, and then told me by signs that if I called out for Mr. Burke (as I was doing) that he would strike me; upon this I got them all in front of the gunyah and fired a revolver over their heads, but they did not seem at all afraid until I got out the gun, when they all ran away. Mr. Burke hearing the report came back, and we saw no more of them until late that night, when they came with some cooked fish and called out 'white fellow.' Mr. Burke then went out with his revolver, and found a whole tribe coming down, all painted, and with fish in small nets carried by two men. Mr. Burke went to meet them, and they wished to surround him; but he knocked as many of the nets of fish out of their hands as he could, and shouted out to me to fire. I did so, and they ran off. We collected five small nets of cooked fish. The reason he would not accept the fish from them was, that he was afraid of being too friendly lest they should be always at our camp. We then lived on fish until Mr. Wills returned. He told us that he had met the natives soon after leaving us, and that they were very kind to him, and had given him plenty to eat both on going up and returning. He seemed to consider that he should have very little difficulty in living with them, and as their camp was close to ours he returned to them the same day and found them very hospitable and friendly, keeping him with them two days. They then made signs to him to be off: he came to us and narrated what had happened, but went back to them the following day, when they gave him his breakfast, but made signs for him to go away; he pretended not to understand them, and would not go, upon which they made signs that they were going up the creek, and that he had better go down: they packed up and left the camp, giving Mr. Wills a little nardoo to take to us.

During his absence, while Mr. Burke was cooking some fish during a strong wind, the flames caught the gunyah and burned so rapidly that we were unable not only to put it out but to save any of our things, excepting one revolver and a gun. Mr. Wills having returned, it was decided to go up the creek and live with the natives if possible, as Mr. Wills thought we should have but little difficulty in obtaining provisions from them if we camped on the opposite side of the creek to them. He said he knew where they were gone, so we packed up and started. Coming to the gunyahs where we expected to have found them, we were disappointed, and seeing a nardoo field close by halted, intending to make it our camp. For some time we were employed gathering nardoo, and laying up a supply. Mr. Wills and I used to collect and carry home a bag each day, and Mr. Burke generally pounded sufficient for our dinner during our absence; but Mr. Wills found himself getting very weak, and was shortly unable to go out to gather nardoo as before, or even strong enough to pound it, so that in a few days he became almost helpless. I still continued gathering, and Mr. Burke now also began to feel very weak, and said he could be of very little use in pounding; I had now to gather and pound for all three of us. I continued to do this for a few days; but finding my strength rapidly failing, my legs being very weak and painful, I was unable to go out for several days, and we were compelled to consume six days' stock which we had laid by. Mr. Burke now proposed that I should gather as much as possible in three days, and that with this supply we should go in search of the natives--a plan which had been urged upon us by Mr. Wills as the only chance of saving him and ourselves as well, as he clearly saw that I was no longer able to collect sufficient for our wants. Raving collected the seed as proposed, and having pounded sufficient to last Mr. Wills for eight days, and two days for ourselves, we placed water and firewood within his reach and started; before leaving him, however, Mr. Burke asked him whether he still wished it, as under no other circumstance would he leave him, and Mr. Wills again said that he looked on it as our only chance. He then gave Mr. Burke a letter and his watch for his father, and we buried the remainder of the field-books near the gunyah. Mr. Wills said that, in case of my surviving Mr. Burke, he hoped that I would carry out his last wishes, iii giving the watch and letter to his father.

In travelling the first day, Mr. Burke seemed very weak, and complained of great pain in his legs and back. On the second day he seemed to be better, and said that he thought he was getting stronger, but on starting, did not go two miles before he said he could go no further. I persisted in his trying to go on, and managed to get him along several times, until I saw that he was almost knocked up, when he said he could not carry his swag, and threw all he had away. I also reduced mine, taking nothing but a gun and some powder and shot, and a small pouch and some matches. In starting again, we did not go far before Mr. Burke said we should halt for the night; but as the place was close to a large sheet of water, and exposed to the wind, I prevailed on him to go a little further, to the next reach of water, where we camped. We searched about and found a few small patches of nardoo, which I collected and pounded, and with a crow, which I shot, made a good evening's meal. From the time we halted Mr. Burke seemed to be getting worse, although he ate his supper; he said he felt convinced he could not last many hours, and gave me his watch, which he said belonged to the committee, and a pocket-book to give to Sir William Stawell, and in which he wrote some notes. He then said to me, 'I hope you will remain with me here till I am quite dead--it is a comfort to know that some one is by; but, when I am dying, it is my wish that you should place the pistol in my right hand, and that you leave me unburied as I lie.' That night he spoke very little, and the following morning I found him speechless, or nearly so, and about eight o'clock he expired. I remained a few hours there, but as I saw there was no use remaining longer I went up the creek in search of the natives. I felt very lonely, and at night usually slept in deserted wurleys belonging to the natives. Two days after leaving the spot where Mr. Burke died, I found some gunyahs where the natives had deposited a bag of nardoo, sufficient to last me a fortnight, and three bundles containing various articles. I also shot a crow that evening; but was in great dread that the natives would come and deprive me of the nardoo.

I remained there two days to recover my strength, and then returned to Mr. Wills. I took back three crows; but found him lying dead in his gunyah, and the natives had been there and had taken away some of his clothes. I buried the corpse with sand, and remained there some days, but finding that my stock of nardoo was running short, and as I was unable to gather it, I tracked the natives who had been to the camp by their footprints in the sand, and went some distance down the creek shooting crows and hawks on the road. The natives, hearing the report of the gun, came to meet me, and took me with them to their camp, giving me nardoo and fish: they took the birds I had shot and cooked them for me, and afterwards showed me a gunyah where I was to sleep with three of the single men. The following morning they commenced talking to me, and putting one finger on the ground and covering it with sand, at the same time pointing up the creek saying 'white fellow,' which I understood to mean that one white man was dead. From this I knew that they were the tribe who had taken Mr. Wills's clothes. They then asked me where the third white man was, and I also made the sign of putting two fingers on the ground and covering them with sand, at the same time pointing up the creek. They appeared to feel great compassion for me when they understood that I was alone on the creek, and gave me plenty to eat. After being four days with them, I saw that they were becoming tired of me, and they made signs that they were going up the creek and that I had better go downwards; but I pretended not to understand them. The same day they shifted camp, and I followed them, and on reaching their camp I shot some arrows, which pleased them so much that they made me a breakwind in the centre of their camp, and came and sat round me until such time as the crows were cooked, when they assisted me to eat them. The same day one of the women, to whom I had given part of a crow, came and gave me a ball of nardoo, saying that she would give me more only she had such a sore arm that she was unable to pound. She showed me a sore on her arm, and the thought struck me that I would boil some water in the billy and wash her arm with a sponge. During the operation, the whole tribe sat round and were muttering one to another. Her husband sat down by her side, and she was crying all the time. After I had washed it, I touched it with some nitrate of silver, when she began to yell, and ran off, crying out 'Mokow! Mokow!' (Fire! Fire!). From this time, she and her husband used to give me a small quantity of nardoo both night and morning, and whenever the tribe was about going on a fishing excursion he used to give me notice to go with them. They also used to assist me in making a wurley or breakwind when-

12

ever they shifted camp. I generally shot a crow or a hawk, and gave it to them in return for these little services. Every four or five days the tribe would surround me and ask whether I intended going up or down the creek; at last I made them understand that if they went up I should go up the creek, and if they went down I should also go down; and from this time they seemed to look upon me as one of themselves, and supplied me with fish and nardoo regularly: they were very anxious, however, to know where Mr. Burke lay, and one day when we were fishing in the waterholes close by, I took them to the spot. On seeing his remains, the whole party wept bitterly, and covered them with bushes. After this, they were much kinder to me than before, and I always told them that the white men would be here before two moons; and in the evening when they came with nardoo and fish they used to talk about the 'white-fellows' coming, at the same time pointing to the moon. I also told them they would receive many presents, and they constantly asked me for tomahawks, called by them. 'Bomay Ko.' From this time to when the relief party arrived, a period of about a month, they treated me with uniform kindness, and looked upon me as one of themselves. The day on which I was released, one of the tribe who had 'been fishing came and told me that the 'white fellows,' were coming, and the whole of the tribe who were then in camp sallied out in every direction to meet the party, while the man who had brought the news took me over the creek, where I shortly-saw the party coming down.

Will's Account of the Dash to the Gulf of Carpentaria

Sunday, 16th December, 1860.--The horse having been shod and our reports finished, we started at 6.40 A.M. for Eyre's Creek, the party consisting of Mr. Burke, myself, King, and Charley, having with us six camels, one horse, and three months' provisions. We followed down the creek to the point where the sandstone ranges cross the creek, and were accompanied to that place by Brahe, who would return to take charge of the depot. Down to this point the banks of the creek are very rugged and stony, but there is a tolerable supply of grass and salt bush in the vicinity. A large tribe of blacks came pestering us to go to their camp and have a dance, which we declined. They were very troublesome, and nothing but the threat to shoot them will keep them away. They are, however, easily frightened; and, although fine-looking men, decidedly not of a warlike disposition. They show the greatest inclination to take whatever they can, but will run no unnecessary risk in so doing. They seldom carry any weapon, except a shield and a large kind of boomerang, which I believe they use for killing rats, etc. Sometimes, but very seldom, they have a large spear; reed spears seem to be quite unknown to them. They are undoubtedly a finer and better-looking race of men than the blacks on the Murray and Darling, and more peaceful; but in other respects I believe they will not compare favourably with them, for from the little we have seen of them, they appear to be mean-spirited and contemptible in every respect.

Monday, 17th December, 1860.--We continued to follow down the creek. Found its course very crooked, and the channel frequently dry for a considerable distance, and then forming into magnificent waterholes, abounding in water fowl of all kinds. The country on each side is more open than on the upper part of the creek. The soil on the plains is of a light earthy nature, supporting abundance of salt bush and grass. Most of the plains are lightly timbered, and the ground is finer and not cracked up as at the head of the creek. Left Camp 67 at ten minutes to six A.M., having breakfasted before leaving. We followed the creek along from point to point, at first in a direction west-north-west for about twelve miles, then about north-west. At about noon we passed the last water, a short distance beyond which the creek runs out on a polygonum* flat (* Polygonum Cunninghami.); but the timber was so large and dense that it deceived us into the belief that there was a continuation of the channel. On crossing the polygonum ground to where we expected to find the creek we became aware of our mistake. Not thinking it advisable to chance the existence of water ahead, we camped at the end of a large but shallow sheet of water in the sandy bed of the creek.

The hole was about 150 links broad, and * (*Blank in original.) feet deep in most places. In many places the temperature of the water was almost incredibly high, which induced me to try it at several points. The mean of two on the shady side of the creek gave 97 4/10 degrees. As may be imagined this water tasted disagreeably warm, but we soon cooled some in water bags, and thinking that it would be interesting to know what we might call cool, I placed the thermometer in a pannikin containing some that appeared delightfully so, almost cold in fact; its temperature was, to our astonishment, 78 degrees. At half-past six, when a strong wind was blowing from south, and temperature of air had fallen to 80 degrees, the lowest temperature of water in the hose, that had been exposed to the full effect of evaporation for several hours was 72 degrees. This water for drinking appeared positively cold, and is too low a temperature to be pleasant under the circumstances. A remarkable southerly squall came on between five and six P.M., with every appearance of rain. The sky however soon cleared, but the wind continued to blow in a squally and irregular manner from the same quarter at evening.

Wednesday, 19th December, 1860.--Started at a quarter-past eight A.M., leaving what seemed to be the end of Cooper's Creek. We took a course a little to the north of west, intending to try and obtain water in some of the creeks that Sturt mentioned that he had crossed, and at the same time to see whether they were connected with Cooper's Creek, as appeared most probable from the direction in which we found the latter running, and from the manner in which it had been breaking up into small channels, flowing across the plains in a north and north-north-west direction. We left on our right the flooded flats on which this branch of the creek runs out, and soon came to a series of sand ridges, the directions of which were between north half-west and north-north-west. The country is well grassed and supports plenty of salt bush. Many of the valleys are liable to be inundated by the overflow of the main creek. They have watercourses and polygonum flats bordered with box trees, but we met with no holes fit to hold a supply of water. At about ten miles we crossed a large earthy flat lightly timbered with box and gum. The ground was very bad for travelling on, being much cracked up and intersected by innumerable channels, which continually carried off the water of a large creek. Some of the valleys beyond this were very pretty, the ground being sound and covered with fresh plants, which made them look beautifully green. At fifteen miles we halted, where two large plains joined. Our attention had been attracted by some red-breasted cockatoos, pigeons, a crow, and several other birds, whose presence made us feel sure that there was water not far off; but our hopes were soon destroyed by finding a claypan just drying up. It contained just sufficient liquid to make the clay boggy. At ten minutes to seven P.M., we moved on, steering straight for Eyre's Creek, north-west by north, intending to make a good night's journey and avoid the heat of the day; but at a mile and a half we came to a creek which looked so well that we followed it for a short distance, and finding two or three waterholes of good milky water we camped for the night. This enabled me to secure an observation of the eclipse of Jupiter's (I) satellite, as well as some latitude observations. The night was so calm that I used the water as an horizon; but I find it much more satisfactory to take the mercury for several reasons.

Thursday, 20th December.--We did not leave this camp until half-past eight, having delayed to refill the water-bags with the milky water, which all of us found to be a great treat again. It is certainly more pleasant to drink than the clear water, and at the same time more satisfying. Our course from here, north-west by north, took us through some pretty country, lightly timbered and well grassed. We could see the line of creek timber winding through the valley on our left. At a distance of five miles there was a bush fire on its banks, and beyond it the creek made a con-siderable bend to the south-west. At two miles farther we came in sight of a large lagoon bearing north by west, and at three miles more we camped on what would seem the same creek as last night, near where it enters the lagoon. The latter is of great extent and contains a large quantity of water, which swarms with wild fowl of every description. It is very shallow, but is sur-rounded by the most pleasing woodland scenery, and everything in the vicinity looks fresh and green. The creek near its junction with the lagoon contains some good waterholes five to six feet deep. They are found in a sandy alluvium which is very boggy when wet. There was a large camp of not less than forty or fifty blacks near where we stopped. They brought us presents of fish, for which we gave them some beads and matches. These fish we found to be a most valuable addition to our rations. They were of the same kind as we had found elsewhere, but finer, being from nine to ten inches long, and two to three inches deep, and in such good condition that they might have been fried in their own fat. It is a remarkable fact, that these were the first blacks who have offered us any fish since we reached Cooper's Creek.

Friday, 21st December.--We left Camp 70 at half-past five A.M., and tried to induce one or two of the blacks to go with us, but it was of no use. Keeping our former course we were pulled up at three miles by a fine lagoon, and then by the creek that flows into it; the latter being full of water, we were obliged to trace it a mile up before we could cross. I observed on its banks two wild plants of the gourd or melon tribe, one much resembling a stunted cucumber: the other, both in leaf and appearance of fruit, was very similar to a small model of a water melon.[1]The latter plant I also found at Camp 68. On tasting the pulp of the newly-found fruit, which was about the size of a large pea, I found it to be so acrid that it was with difficulty that I removed the taste from my mouth. At eight or nine miles from where we crossed the creek we passed another large lagoon, leaving it two miles on our left, and shortly afterwards we saw one nearly as far on our right. This last we should have availed ourselves of, but that we expected to find water in a creek which we could see, by the timber lining its banks, flowed from the lagoon on our left and crossed our course a few miles ahead. We reached it at a distance of four or five miles farther, and found a splendid waterhole at which we camped. The creek at the point flows in a northerly direction through a large lightly timbered flat, on which it partially runs out. The ground is, however, sound and well clothed with grass and salsolaceous plants. Up to this point the country through which we have passed has been of the finest description for pastoral purposes. The grass and salt-bush are everywhere abundant, and water is plentiful with every appearance of permanence. We met with porcupine grass,[2] and only two sand ridges before reaching Camp 71.

Saturday, 22nd December.--At five minutes to five A.M. we left one of the most delightful camps we have had in the journey, and proceeded on the same course as before, north-west by north, across some high ridges of loose sand, many of which

---

[1] Probably Muckia micrantha.--F.M.
[2] Triodia pungens.--Br.

were partially clothed with porcupine grass. We found the ground much worse to travel over than any we have yet met with, as the ridges were exceedingly abrupt and steep on their eastern side, and although sloping gradually towards the west, were so honeycombed in some places by the burrows of rats, that the camels were continually in danger of falling. At a distance of about six miles, we descended from these ridges to undulating country of open box forest, where everything was green and fresh. There is an abundance of grass and salt bushes, and lots of birds of all descriptions. Several flocks of pigeons passed over our heads, making for a point a little to our right, where there is no doubt plenty of water, but we did not go off our course to look for it. Beyond the box forest, which keeps away to the right, we again entered the sand ridges, and at a distance of six miles, passed close to a dry salt lagoon, the ridges in the vicinity of which are less regular in their form and direction, and contain nodules of limestone. The ground in the flats and claypans near, has that encrusted surface that cracks under the pressure of the foot, and is a sure indication of saline deposits. At a distance of eight miles from the lagoon, we camped at the foot of a sand ridge, jutting out on the stony desert. I was rather disappointed, but not altogether surprised, to find the latter nothing more nor less than the stony rises that we had before met with, only on a larger scale and not quite as undulating. During the afternoon several crows came to feed on the plain. They came from an east-north-east direction, no doubt from a portion of the creek that flows through the forest that we left on our right. In the morning, as we were loading, a duck passed over, but it was too dark to see which way it went.

Sunday, 23rd December.--At five A.M. we struck out across the desert in a west-north-west direction. At four and a-half miles we crossed a sand ridge, and then returned to our north-west by north course. We found the ground not nearly as bad for travelling on as that between Bulloo and Cooper's Creek. In fact I do not know whether it arose from our exaggerated anticipation of horrors or not, but we thought it far from bad travelling ground, and as to pasture it is only the actually stony ground that is bare, and many a sheep run is in fact worse grazing ground than that. At fifteen miles we crossed another sand ridge, for several miles round which there is plenty of grass and fine salt bush. After crossing this ridge we descended to an earthy plain, where the ground was rather heavy, being in some places like pieces of slaked lime, and intersected by small watercourses; flocks of pigeons rose from amongst the salt bushes and polygonum; but all the creeks were dry, although marked by lines of box timber. Several gunyahs of the blacks were situated near a waterhole that had apparently contained water very lately, and heaps of grass were lying about the plains, from which they had beaten the seeds. We pushed on, hoping to find the creeks assuming an improved appearance, but they did not, and at one o'clock we halted, intending to travel through part of the night. About sunset, three flocks of pigeons passed over us, all going in the same direction, due north by compass, and passing over a ridge of sand in that direction. Not to have taken notice of such an occurrence would have been little short of a sin, so we determined to go eight or ten miles in that direction. Starting at seven o'clock P.M., we, at six miles, crossed the ridge over which the birds had flown, and came on a flat, subject to inundation. The ground was at first hard and even like the bottom of a claypan, but at a mile or so, we came on cracked earthy ground, intersected by numberless small channels running in all directions. At nine miles we reached the bed of a creek running from east to west: it was only bordered by polygonum bushes, but as there was no timber visible on the plains, we thought it safer to halt until daylight, for fear we should miss the water. At daylight, when we had saddled, a small quantity of timber could be seen at the point of a sand ridge about a mile and a half or two miles to the west of us, and on going there we found a fine creek, with a splendid sheet of water more than a mile long, and averaging nearly three chains broad: it is, however, only two or three feet deep in most parts.

Monday, 24th December, 1860.--We took a day of rest on Gray's Creek to celebrate Christmas. This was doubly pleasant, as we had never, in our most sanguine moments, anticipated finding such a delightful oasis in the desert. Our camp was really an agreeable place, for we had all the advantages of food and water, attending a position of a large creek or river, and were at the same time free from the annoyance of the numberless ants, flies, and mosquitoes that are invariably met with amongst timber or heavy scrub.

Tuesday, 25th December, 1860.--We left Gray's Creek at half-past four A.M. and proceeded to cross the earthy rotten plains in the direction of Eyre's Creek. At a distance of about nine miles we reached some lines of trees and bushes which were visible from the top of the sand ridge at Gray's Creek. We found them growing on the banks of several small creeks which trend to the north and north-north-west; at a mile and a half further we crossed a small creek north-north-east, and joining the ones above mentioned. This creek contained abundance of water in small detached holes from fifty to a hundred links long, well shaded by steep banks and overhanging bushes. The water had a suspiciously transparent colour and a slight trace of brackishness, but the latter was scarcely perceptible. Near where the creek joined the holes is a sandhill and a dense mass of fine timber. The smoke of a fire indicated the presence of blacks, who soon made their appearance and followed us for some distance, beckoning us away to the north-east. We however continued our course north-west by north, but at a distance of one mile and a half found that the creek did not come round as we expected, and that the fall of the water was in a direction nearly opposite to our course, or about west to east. We struck off north half west for a high sand ridge, from which we anticipated seeing whether it were worth while for us to follow the course of the creeks we had crossed. We were surprised to find all the watercourses on the plains trending rather to the south of east, and at a distance of three miles, after changing our course, and when we approached the sandhills towards which we had been steering, we were

21

agreeably pulled up by a magnificent creek coming from the north-north-west, and running in the direction of the fire we had seen. We had now no choice but to change our course again, for we could not have crossed even if we had desired to do so. On following up the south bank of the creek we found it soon keeping a more northerly course than it had where we first struck it. This fact, together with its magnitude and general appearance, lessened the probability of its being Eyre's Creek, as seemed at first very likely from their relative positions and directions. The day being very hot and the camels tired from travelling over the earthy plains, which by-the-by are not nearly so bad as those at the head of Cooper's Creek, we camped at one P.M., having traced the creek up about five miles, not counting the bends. For the whole of this distance we found not a break or interruption of water, which appears to be very deep; the banks are from twenty to thirty feet above the water, and very steep; they are clothed near the water's edge with mint and other weeds, and on the top of each side there is a belt of box trees and various shrubs. The lower part of the creek is bounded towards the north by a high red sand ridge, and on the south side is an extensive plain, intersected by numerous watercourses, which drain off the water in flood-time. The greater portion of the plain is at present very bare, but the stalks of dry grass show that after rain or floods there will be a good crop on the harder and well drained portion; but I believe the loose earthy portion supports no vegetation at any time. The inclination of the ground from the edge of the creek-bank towards the plain is in many places very considerable; this I should take to indicate that the flooding is or has been at one time both frequent and regular.

Wednesday, 26th December, 1860.--We started at five A.M., following up the creek from point to point of the bends. Its general course was at first north-by-west, but at about six miles, the sand ridge on the west closed in on it, and at this point it takes a turn to the north-north-east for half a mile, and then comes around suddenly north-west. Up to this point it had been rather improving in appearance than otherwise, but in the bend to the north-west. the channel is very broad. Its bed being lime-stone rock and indurated clay, is for a space of five or six chains quite dry; then commences another waterhole, the creek keeping a little more towards north. We crossed the creek here and struck across the plain in a due northerly course, for we could see the line of timber coming up to the sand ridges in that direction. For from seven to eight miles we did not touch the creek, and the eastern sand ridge seceded to a distance, in some places of nearly three miles, from our line, leaving an immense extent of grassy plain between it and the creek. The distinctly marked feature on the lower part of this creek is that whenever the main creek is on one side of a plain, there is always a fine billibong on the opposite side, each of them almost invariably sticking close to the respective sand ridges. Before coming to the next bend of the creek a view from the top of a sandhill showed me that the creek received a large tributary from the north-west at about two miles above where we had crossed it. A fine line of timber, running up to the north-west, joined an extensive tract of box forest, and the branch we were following was lost to view in a similar forest towards the north. The sand ridge was so abrupt when we came to the creek, that it was necessary to descend into its bed through one of the small ravines adjoining it. We found it partially run out, the bed being sand and strewed with nodules of lime, some of which were from one half to two feet long: they had apparently been formed in the sanddowns by infiltration.

Sunday, 30th December, 1860.--Finding that the creek was trending considerably towards the east without much likelihood of altering its course, we struck off from it, taking a ten days' supply of water, as there were ranges visible to the north, which had the appearance of being stony. A northeast by northerly course was first taken for about seven miles in order to avoid them. The whole of this distance was over alluvial earthy plains, the soil of which was firm, but the vegetation scanty.

Saturday, 5th January, 1861.--On leaving Camp 84, we found slight but distinct indications of rain in the groves, and a few blades of grass and small weeds in the little depressions on the plain: these indications were, however, so slight, that, but for the fact of our having found surface-water in two holes near our camp, we should hardly have noticed them. At a distance of about two miles in a north-north-easterly direction, we came to a creek with a long broad shallow waterhole. The well-worn paths, the recent tracks of natives, and the heaps of shells, on the contents of which the latter had feasted, showed at once that this creek must be connected with some creek of considerable importance. The camels and horses being greatly in need of rest, we only moved up about half a mile, and camped for the day.

Sunday, 6th January, 1861.--Started at twenty minutes to six o'clock, intending to make an easy day's stage along the creek. As we proceeded up in a northerly direction, we found the waterhole to diminish in size very much, and at about two and a half miles the creek ran out in a lot of small watercourses. At the upper end of the creek we found in its bed what appeared to be an arrangement for catching fish: it consisted of a small oval mud paddock about twelve feet by eight feet, the sides of which were about nine inches above the bottom of the hole, and the top of the fence covered with long grass, so arranged that the ends of the blades overhung scantily by several inches the sides of the hole. As there was no sign of timber to the north, we struck off to north-west by north for a fine line that came up from south-west, and seemed to run parallel with the creek we were about to leave. At a distance of about three miles, we reached the bank of a fine creek containing a sheet of water two chains broad, and at least fifteen feet deep in the middle. The banks are shelving, sandy, and lightly clothed with box trees and various shrubs. On starting to cross the plains towards this creek we were surprised at the bright green appearance of strips of land, which look in the distance like swamps. On approaching some of them, we found that there had been a considerable fall of rain in some places, which had raised a fine crop of grass and portulac[3] wherever the soil was of a sandy and light nature; but the amount of moisture

---

[3] Portulaca oleracea. L.

had been insufficient to affect the hard clayey ground which constitutes the main portion of the plain. The sight of two native companions feeding here, added greatly to the encouraging prospects; they are the only specimens of that bird that I remember to have seen on that side of the Darling.

7th January, 1861.--We started at half-past four A.M. without water, thinking that we might safely rely on this creek for one day's journey. We, however, found the line of timber soon begin to look small; at three miles the channel contained only a few pools of surface water. We continued across the plains on a due northerly course, frequently crossing small watercourses, which had been filled by the rain, but were fast drying up. Here and there, as we proceeded, dense lines of timber on our right showed that the creek came from the east of north; at a distance of thirteen miles we turned to the north-north-east towards a fine line of timber. We found a creek of considerable dimensions, that had only two or three small waterholes, but as there was more than sufficient for us, and very little feed for the beasts anywhere else, we camped. I should have liked this camp to have been in a more prominent and easily recognizable position, as it happens to be almost exactly on the tropic of Capricorn. The tremendous gale of wind that we had in the evening and night prevented me from taking a latitude observation, whereas I had some good ones at the last camp and at Camp 87. My reckoning cannot be far out. I found, on taking out my instruments, that one of the spare thermometers was broken, and the glass of my aneroid barometer cracked; the latter I believe not otherwise injured. This was done by the camel having taken it into his head to roll while the pack was on his back.

Tuesday, 8th January, 1861.--Started at a quarter past five A.M. with a load of water, determined to be independent of all creeks and watercourses. At a mile and a half, found surface water in a small creek, and at a mile farther, water in two or three places on the open plains. The country we crossed for the first ten miles consists of fine open plains of firm argillaceous soils, too stiff and hard to be affected by the small quantity of rain that has fallen as yet. They are subject to inundations from the overflow of a number of small creeks, which intersect them in a direction east-north-east to west-south-west. Nearly all the creeks are lined with box trees and shrubs in a tolerably healthy state; of the remains of dead trees there is only a fair proportion to the living ones. After traversing a plain of greater extent than the rest, we, at ten miles, reached the creek, proportionately large and important looking. The channel, however, at the point where we struck it, was deep, level, and dry; but I believe there is water in it not far off, for there were some red-breasted cockatoos in the trees, and native parrots on each side. On the north side there is a part bearing off to the north-north-west. The mirage on the plain to the south of the creek was stronger than I have before seen it. There appear to be sheets of water within a few yards of one, and it looks sufficiently smooth and glassy to be used for an artificial horizon. To the westward of the plains, some fine sandhills were visible, nearly in the direction in which the creek flowed. To the north of the creek the country undergoes a great change. At first there is a little earthy land subject to inundation. The soil then becomes more sandy, with stony pans in which water collects after rain; the whole country is slightly undulating, lightly timbered, and splendidly grassed. A number of small disconnected creeks are scattered about, many of which contained water protected from the sun and wind by luxuriant growth of fine grasses and small bushes. We passed one or two little rises of sand and pebbles, on which were growing some trees quite new to me; but for the seed pods I should have taken them for a species of Casuarina, although the leaf-stalks have not the jointed peculiarities of those plants. The trunks and branches are like the she oak, the leaves like those of a pine; they droop like a willow, and the seed is small, flat, in a large flat pod, about six inches by three-quarters of an inch. As we proceeded, the country improved at every step. Flocks of pigeons rose and flew off to the eastward, and fresh plants met our view on every rise; everything green and luxuriant. The horse licked his lips, and tried all he could to break his nose-string in order to get at the food. We camped at the foot of a sandy rise, where there was a large stony pan with plenty of water, and where the feed was equal in quality, and superior as to variety, to any that I have seen in Australia, excepting perhaps on some soils of volcanic origin.

Wednesday, 9th January, 1861.--Started at five minutes past five, without water, trusting to get a supply of water from the rain that fell during the thunderstorm. Traversed six miles of undulating plains covered with vegetation richer than ever. Several ducks rose from the little creeks as we passed, and flocks of pigeons were flying in all directions. The richness of the vegetation is evidently not suddenly arising from chance thunderstorms, for the trees and bushes on the open plain are everywhere healthy and fresh looking; very few dead ones are to be seen; besides which, the quantity of dead and rotten grass which at present almost overpowers in some places the young blades shows that this is not the first crop of the kind. The grasses are numerous and many of them unknown to me, but they only constitute a moderate portion of the herbage. Several kinds of spurious vetches and portulac, as well as salsolaceae, add to the luxuriance of the vegetation. At seven miles we found ourselves in an open forest country, where the feed was good, but not equal to what we had passed, neither had it been visited by yesterday's rain. We soon emerged again on open plains, but the soil being of a more clayish nature, they were not nearly so much advanced in vegetation as the others. We found surface water in several places, and at one spot disturbed a fine bustard which was feeding in the long grass; we did not see him until he flew up. I should have mentioned that one flew over our camp last evening in a northerly direction; this speaks well for the country and climate. At noon we came to a large creek the course of which was from east-north-east to west-south-west; the sight of the white gum trees in the distance had raised hopes, which were not at all damped on a close inspection of the channel. At the point where we struck it there was certainly no great quantity of water; the bed was broad and sandy, but its whole appearance was that of an important watercourse, and the large gums which line its banks, together with the improved appearance of the soil, and the abundance of feed in the vicinity, satisfied us as to the permanency of the water and the value of the discovery. Although it was so early in the day, and we were anxious to make a good march, yet we camped here, as it seemed to be almost a sin to leave such good quarters. The bed of the creek is loose sand, through which the water freely permeates; it is, however, sufficiently coarse not to be boggy, and animals can approach the water without any difficulty.

Thursday, 10th January, 1861.--At twenty minutes past five A.M., we left our camp with a full supply of water, determined to risk no reverses, and to make a good march. I should mention that last evening we had been nearly deafened by the noise of the cicadariae, and but for our large fires should have been kept awake all night by the mosquitoes. A walk of two miles across a well grassed plain brought us to a belt of timber, and we soon afterwards found ourselves pulled up by a large creek in which the water was broad and deep; we had to follow up the bank of the creek in a north-easterly direction for nearly a mile before we could cross, when to our joy we found that it was flowing; not a muddy stream from the effects of recent floods, but a small rivulet of pure water as clear as crystal. The bed of the river at this place is deep and rather narrow; the water flows over sand and pebbles, winding its way between clumps of melalema, and gum saplings. After leaving the river, we kept our old course due north, crossing, at a distance of one mile, three creeks with gum trees on their banks. The soil of the flats through which they flow is a red loam of fair quality and well grassed. Beyond the third creek is a large plain, parts of which are very stony, and this is bounded towards the east by a low stony rise, partly composed of decayed and honeycombed quartz rock in situ, and partly of waterworn pebbles and other alluvial deposits. At about two miles across this plain, we reached the first of a series of small creeks with deep waterholes: these creeks and holes have the characteristics peculiar to watercourses which are found in flats formed from the alluvial deposits of schistose rocks. The banks are on a level with the surrounding ground, and are irregularly marked by small trees, or only by tufts of long grass which overhang the channel and frequently bide it from one's view, even when within a few yards. At about five miles from where we crossed the river, we came to the main creek in these flats, Patten's Creek; it flows along at the foot of a stony range, and we had to trace it up nearly a mile in a north-north-easterly direction before we could cross it; as it happened, we might almost as well have followed its course up the flat, for at a little more than two miles we came to it again. We re-crossed it at a stony place just below a very large waterhole, and then continued our course over extensive plains, not so well grassed as those we had passed before, and very stony in some places. At eight miles from Patten's Creek, we came to another, running from south-west to south-east there was plenty of water in it, but it was evidently the result of recent local rains. On the banks was an abundance of good feed but very little timber.

Friday, 11th January, 1861.--We started at five A.M., and in the excitement of exploring fine well-watered country, forgot all about the eclipse of the sun until the reduced temperature and peculiarly gloomy appearance of the sky drew our attention to the matter; it was then too late to remedy the deficiency, so we made a good day's journey, the moderation of the midday heat, which was only about 86 degrees, greatly assisting us. The country traversed has the most verdant and cheerful aspect; abundance of feed and water everywhere. All the creeks seen to-day have a course more or less to the east by south. The land improves in appearance at every mile. A quantity of rain has fallen here and to the south, and some of the flats are suitable for cultivation, if the regularity of the seasons will admit.

Saturday, 12th January, 1861.--We started at five A.M., and, keeping as nearly as possible a due northerly course, traversed for about eight miles a splendid flat, through which flow several fine well-watered creeks, lined with white gum trees. We then entered a series of slaty, low, sandstone ranges, amongst which were some well-grassed flats, and plenty of water in the main gullies. The more stony portions are, however, covered with porcupine grass, and here and there with mallee; large ant-hills are very numerous; they vary in height from two and a half to four feet. There was a continuous rise perceptible all the way in crossing the ranges, and from the highest portion, which we reached at a distance of about seven miles, we had a pretty good view of the country towards the north. As far as we could see in the distance, and bearing due north, was a large range, having somewhat the outline of a granite mountain. The east end of this range just comes up to the magnetic north; on the left of this, and bearing north-north-west, is a single conical peak, the top of which only is visible. Further to the west there were some bro-ken ranges, apparently sandstone; to the east of north the tops of very distant and apparently higher ranges were seen, the outline of which was so indistinct that I can form no idea as to their character; the intermediate country below us appeared alterna-tions of fine valleys and stony ranges, such as we had just been crossing. From here a descent of two miles brought us to a creek having a northern course, but on tracing it down for about a mile, we found it to turn to the southeast and join another from the north. We crossed over to the latter on a north-by-westerly course, and camped on the west bank. It has a broad sandy chan-nel; the waterholes are large, but not deep; the banks are bordered with fine white gums, and are in some places very scrubby. There is abundance of rich green feed everywhere in the vicinity. We found here numerous indications of blacks hav-ing been here, but saw nothing of them. It seems remarkable that where their tracks are so plentiful, we should have seen none since we left King's Creek. I observed that the natives here climb trees as those on the Murray do, in search of some animal corre-sponding in habits to the opossum, which they get out of the hollow branches in a similar manner. I have not yet been able to ascertain what the animal is.

Sunday, 13th January, 1861.--We did not leave camp this morning until half-past seven, having delayed for the purpose of getting the camels' shoes on--a matter in which we were eminently unsuccessful. We took our breakfast before starting, for almost the first time since leaving the depot. Having crossed the creek, our course was due north as before, until, at about six miles, we came in sight of the range ahead, when we took a north-half-easterly direction for the purpose of clearing the eastern front of it. We found the ground more sandy than what we had before crossed, and a great deal of it even more richly grassed. Camp 93 is situate at the junction of three sandy creeks, in which there is abundance of water. The sand is loose, and the water permeates freely, so that the latter may be obtained delightfully cool and clear by sinking anywhere in the beds of the creeks.

Saturday, 19th January, 1861.--Started from Camp 98 at 530 A.M., and passing to the north-west of Mount Forbes, across a fine and well-grassed plain, kept at first a north-by-easterly direction. At a distance of three miles, the plain became everywhere stony, being scattered over with quartz pebbles; and a little further on we came to low quartz ranges, the higher portions of which are covered with porcupine grass, but the valleys are well clothed with a variety of coarse and rank herbage. At about five miles we crossed a creek with a sandy bed, which has been named Green's Creek; there were blacks not far above where we crossed, but we did not disturb them. After crossing the creek, we took a due northerly course over very rugged quartz ranges of an auriferous character. Pieces of iron ore, very rich, were scattered in great numbers over some of the hills. On our being about to cross one of the branch creeks in the low range, we surprised some blacks--a man who, with a young fellow apparently his son, was upon a tree, cutting out something; and a lubra with a piccaninny. The two former did not see me until I was nearly close to them, and then they were dreadfully frightened; jumping down from the trees, they started off, shouting what sounded to us very like 'Joe, Joe.' Thus disturbed, the lubra, who was at some distance from them, just then caught sight of the camels and the remainder of the party as they came over the hill into the creek, and this tended to hasten their flight over the stones and porcupine grass. Crossing the range at the head of this creek, we came on a gully running north, down which we proceeded, and soon found it open out into a creek, at two or three points in which we found water. On this creek we found the first specimen of an eucalyptus, which has a very different appearance from the members of the gum-tree race. It grows as high as a good-sized gum tree, but with the branches less spreading: in shape it much resembles the elm; the foliage is dark, like that of the light wood; the trunk and branches are covered with a grey bark resembling in outward appearance that of the box tree. Finding that the creek was trending too much to the eastward, we struck off to the north again, and at a short distance came on a fine creek running about south-south-east. As it was now nearly time to camp, we travelled it up for about one and a-half mile, and came to a fine waterhole in a rocky basin, at which there were lots of birds.

Sunday, 27th January, 1861.--Started from Camp 105 at five minutes past two in the morning. We followed along the bends of the creek by moonlight, and found the creek wind about very much, taking on the whole a north-easterly course. At about five miles it changed somewhat its features; from a broad and sandy channel, winding about through gum-tree flats, it assumes the unpropitious appearance of a straight, narrow creek, running in a north-north-easterly direction between high, perpendicular, earthy banks. After running between three or four miles in this manner, it took a turn to the west, at which point there is a fine waterhole, and then assumed its original character. Below this we found water at several places, but it all seemed to be either from surface drainage or from springs in the sand. The land in the vicinity of the creek appears to have received plenty of rain, the vegetation everywhere green and fresh; but there is no appearance of the creek having flowed in this part of the channel for a considerable period. Palm trees are numerous, and some bear an abundance of small, round dates (nuts) just ripening. These palms give a most picturesque and pleasant appearance to the creek.

Wednesday, 30th January, 1861.--Started at half-past seven A.M., after several unsuccessful attempts at getting Golah out of the bed of the creek. It was determined to try bringing him down until we could find a place for him to get out at; but after going in this way two or three miles it was found necessary to leave him behind, as it was almost impossible to get him through some of the waterholes, and had separated King from the party, which became a matter for very serious consideration when we found blacks hiding in the box trees close to us.

Sunday, February, 1861.--Finding the ground in such a state from the heavy falls of rain, that camels could scarcely be got along, it was decided to leave them at Camp 119, and for Mr. Burke and I to proceed towards the sea on foot. After breakfast we accordingly started, taking with us the horse and three days' provisions. Our first difficulty was in crossing Billy's Creek, which we had to do where it enters the river, a few hundred yards below the camp. In getting the horse in here, he got bogged in a quicksand bank so deeply as to be unable to stir, and we only succeeded in extricating him by undermining him on the creek's side, and then lugging him into the water. Having got all the things in safety, we continued down the river bank, which bent about from east to west, but kept a general northerly course. A great deal of the land was so soft and rotten that the horse, with only a saddle and about twenty-five pounds on his back, could scarcely walk over it. At a distance of about five miles we again had him bogged in crossing a small creek, after which he seemed so weak that we had great doubts about getting him on. We, however, found some better ground close to the water's edge, where the sandstone rock crops out, and we stuck to it as far as possible. Finding that the river was bending about so much that we were making very little progress in a northerly direction, we struck off due north and soon came on some table-land, where the soil is shallow and gravelly, and clothed with box and swamp gums. Patches of the land were very boggy, but the main portion was sound enough; beyond this we came on an open plain, covered with water up to one's ankles. The soil here was a stiff clay, and the surface very uneven, so that between the tufts of grass one was frequently knee deep in water. The bottom, however, was sound and no fear of bogging. After floundering through this for several miles, we came to a path formed by the blacks, and there were distinct signs of a recent migration in a southerly direction. By making use of this path we got on much better, for the ground was well trodden and bard. At rather more than a mile, the path entered a forest through which flowed a nice watercourse, and we had not gone far before we found places where the blacks had been camping. The forest was inter-sected by little pebbly rises, on which they had made their fires, and in the sandy ground adjoining some of the former had been digging yams, which seemed to be so numerous that they could afford to leave lots of them about, probably having only selected the 'very best. We were not so particular, but ate many of those that they had rejected, and found them very good. About half a mile further, we came close on a black fellow, who was coiling up by a camp fire, whilst his gin and piccaninny were yabbering alongside. We stopped for a short time to take out some of the pistols that were on the horse, and that they might see us before we were so near as to frighten them. Just after we stopped, the black got up to stretch his limbs, and after a few seconds looked in our direction. It was very amusing to see the way in which he stared, standing for some time as if he thought he must be dreaming, and then, having signalled to the others, they dropped on their haunches, and shuffled off in the quietest manner possi-ble. Near their fire was a fine hut, the best I have ever seen, built on the same principle as those at Cooper's Creek, but much lar-ger and more complete I should say a dozen blacks might comfortably coil in it together. It is situated at the end of the for-est towards the north, and looks out on an extensive marsh, which is at times flooded by the sea water. Hundreds of wild geese, plover and pelicans, were enjoying themselves in the watercourses on the marsh, all the water on which was too brackish to be drinkable, except some holes that are filled by the stream that flows through the forest. The neighbourhood of this encampment is one of the prettiest we have seen during the journey. Proceeding on our course across the marsh, we came to a channel through which the sea water enters. Here we passed three blacks, who, as is universally their custom, pointed out to us, unasked, the best part down. This assisted us greatly, for the ground we were taking was very boggy. We moved slowly down about three miles and then camped for the night; the horse Billy being completely baked. Next morning we started at daybreak, leaving the horse short hobbled.

Part Two:
Journal of Expedition
in Search of Burke and Wills

by
Frederick Walker

Introduction

Frederick Walker, [the author of the following journal], was born in England around 1820 and died of gulf fever in Floraville, Queensland on 19 September 1866.

Walker emigrated to Australia as a young man. He held the position of Clerk of Petty Sessions in Tumut, NSW, before he was appointed as the first Commandant of the Native Police on the recommendation of William Charles Wentworth and Augustus Morris, two members of the Legislative Council.

As Commandant of the Corps of Native Police, Walker was spectacularly successsful ending the depradations of the Bigambul people in the Macintyre district.

In 1861 Walker led a party in search of the ill fated Burke and Wills expedition and kept a meticulous journal of the search. Walker's Creek, located near Marathon Station in far north Queensland is named after Frederick Walker.

Frederick Walker's grave is located 71 kilometers south of the township on Floraville Station, in far north Queensland. The inscription reads:

"On August 17 1848 Frederick Walker, aged 28, was appointed to the position of Commandant of the Corps of Native Police having emigrated from Australia from England. The Corps commenced with fourteen troopers recruited from four different New South Wales tribes. In 1850 Walker had three units and two lieutenants in the corps and by 1852 he increased the Corps with 48 additional Aboriginal troopers who were drilled and trained in the use of carbines, swords, saddles and bridles. The Native Mounted Police Corps were responsible for maintaining law and order beyond the settled districts. On 12 October 1854 Walker was dismissed from the service for impropriety of conduct due to his heavy drinking. After his dismissal he continued to live on the frontier and briefly formed an illegal force of ten ex-troopers from the Native Police Corps to protect settlers in the Upper Dawson region. In August of 1861 fears had grown for the safety of the Burke and Wills expedition and Walker was sent at the insistence of the Royal Society of Victoria to search for the ill-fated expedition.

"Frederick Walker was in many ways a remarkable man. His exploration of the Gulf assisted in opening up the region and his maps were considered accurate. Walker did not find Burke and Wills but he did find Camp 119, the last Burke and Wills camp before they turned south on their return journey. After lengthy explorations of the Gulf region Walker was then employed by the Superintendant of Electric Telegraph to survey a 500 mile route from Bowen to Burketown in a bid to compete against South Australia to have Burketown the end of the Trans-Oceanic link from Europe. Although Frederick Walker lost the race and Darwin became the terminus. He did survey the line. He arrived in Burketown with his party of four Europeans and four Aboriginal assistants at the height of the Gulf Fever - a typhoid which affected the Gulf after the arrival in Burketown of a vessel on which all the crew except the Captain died. Walker commenced his return journey but at Floraville he became ill and after several days he also died of the Gulf Fever on 19 September 1866. The entry in the expedition's logbook recorded the passing of a pioneer of the gulf: 'as soon as the horses were brought up and a couple saddled Perrier and Ewan were starting for the doctor of the Leichhardt search expedition which was camped about six miles off. But he (Walker) died before they mounted. He died at noon and was buried on the evening of the same day. So ended the life of a remarkable Australian."

September, 1861

This journal by Frederick Walker, 'Expedition in search of Burke and Wills,' was extracted from pages 133-150 of The Journal of the Royal Geographical Society *(vol. 33) 1863, and was edited by the Assistant-Secretary with maps and illustrations (London: John Murray, Albemarle Street).*

Journal of Mr. Walker from the day he left Macintosh's Station, on the Nogoa, to that of his arrival at the Albert River, Gulf of Carpentaria.

On the 15th Sept., [1861] left Mr. Macintosh's station on a creek flowing into the Nogoa, which I crossed on the 19th, and then went to the north to hit Poma, which tributary of the Claude takes its rise at my pass over the main range; this is a great detour, but by this means I avoided the dense brigalow scrub which intervenes between the Nogoa River and Salvator Lake and the pass. On the 20th we reached the beautiful Emerald Downs, on Poma Creek, camped there the 21st, and arrived at the foot of the pass and my old camp on the 23rd; the grass had caught fire from my camp, and was now a fine sward. We camped on the Nivelle the 25th. My first marked tree is on Emerald Downs, as that was new ground to me. The 26th we pushed down to the Nive, about 5 miles above my old No. 11 camp. The next day, 27th, crossed over to the Victoria, and camped (No. 6) below my No. 29 tree. On the 28th, 29th, and 30th, pushed down the Victoria by fair stages, and on the morning of the 7th October found Camp 10 was in long. 146° 1' E., lat. 24° 34' S. Whilst camped here we searched for the L tree seen by Gregory; but as we had seen his 22nd (XXIL) tree on the north bank, we searched on the same for the L tree and it was not until the 5th Jingle and Mr. Haughton found it on the south bank. In the meanwhile I had found another L tree 2 miles below our camp on north side, and 7 below the tree seen by Gregory. I looked for an open road N.N.W., but was checked by a dense, almost impenetrable scrub of acacia. Mitchell calls this acacia "brigalow," but that is incorrect, for it differs much from it, and I have seen but two or three real brigalow since we crossed the ridge dividing the Nive watershed from that of the Victoria. The blacks call this acacia "gurrt." Brigalow they call "noorwool." A little below the second L tree, I found I could pass round the termination of this scrub. I surmise that Leichhardt intended leaving the Victoria at the tree seen by Gregory; was stopped in his N.N.W. course by the same barrier encountered by me, and turned back to camp at the tree found by me, subsequently clearing the scrub where I rounded it. His track, if he had dry weather, would, on this basaltic soil, be soon obliterated.

October, 1861

October 7.--There was much difficulty in catching the horses this morning, owing to their having improved so much during the last few days' spell. Passed by Leichhardt's second L tree; thence over a succession of downs and plains, intersected by narrow and open scrub of the acacia the blacks call "gurrt." Rain at night. Distance, 17 miles.

Oct. 8.--Course still N.N.W. Crossed a sandy creek with large bed, but no water; it was here running through sand-hills, but lower down I could see it opened on the downs and plains we had been traversing all morning. One mile beyond this we killed an emeu. Passed another creek, with a pool of water, luckily for the horses. We now ascended a high downs ridge, surmounted by a belt of scrub. Still N.N.W. We had reached the division of waters betwixt the Alice and Victoria. The first creek crossed to-day was no doubt that crossed by Sir Thomas Mitchell, arid which he marks on his map as a deep rocky channel. Last 5½ miles was through sandy box country, clothed with a grass like knitting-needles. Camped without water at dusk. Distance, 20½ miles.

Oct. 9.--Shortly after starting we found a pool of muddy or rather milky-looking water; the horses indulged in a good drink, and we filled two of our excellent water-bags--last night we found the benefit of them. I now turned to my course again N.N.W., which we followed till I discerned symptoms of a watercourse trending N. by E. 10°. A very short distance showed I was right, and I followed it through a scrub to where it joined a larger creek, which flowed W.N.W. This creek I followed to camp (No. 13), at a place sufficiently open and well grassed for my purpose. This creek had, after we came on it, received two tributaries from the north-east, and had now abundance of water, possibly, but not certainly, permanent. Except the last 6 miles, the ground was the same sandy box country, with the same grass, as yesterday evening.--Distance, 16 miles.

Oct. 10.--To-day travelled over a tableland of sandy ground, with the same needle-like grass as yesterday. Then descended into a broad sandy creek, with reeds, and which bad not long ceased running; I called this the Patrick, after one of my old comrades (aboriginal). The Patrick now ran N.N.W. 30°, and then N.N.W. 25°; I therefore followed it till it turned N.W. 45°; but I still followed it, for the heavy sandy ground and an oppressively hot day I saw was distressing to the horses; at the end of another 2 miles it turned N.N.W. 25°, when a half-mile's ride brought us to a long reach of water, at which I camped, as the day's work was too much broken into. Camp No. 14 is about 9 miles from the Alice. When I left the Victoria, I laid down in pencil, on Mitchell's map, what I supposed to be the probable course of the Alice, also a tributary which exactly answers to the creek we were on last night, and which I have now called the Macalister. The Patrick I fell in with 3 miles sooner than I anticipated, but its northerly course makes up for that. I hope to fall in on the other side of the Alice with a tributary coming from the N.N.W., possibly from the north. The advance party to-day saw very old tracks of horses, and apparently mules, going down the Patrick. I much regret not having seen them, as they must have been Leichhardt's. Distance, 11 miles.

Oct. 11.--Started Mr. Macalister, with instructions to travel N.N.W. by compass. I pulled him up at a beautiful camp, on a small creek, with excellent grass. The country, after the first 4 miles, was all plains and downs, intersected by small belts of the gurrt (acacia) scrub. The last 5 miles were over very fine downs, clothed with that excellent grass I call rye (because it always grows near barley-grass). From these downs I saw the range, about 25 miles to the east. Distance, 9 miles (presumed).

Oct. 12.--To-day we rode N.N.W. by compass, over fine very high downs; crossed two small creeks flowing from them N. by W., and camped at the head of a third. The range now lay about 20 miles east, and betwixt us and it there was a fine downy valley, evidently well watered. Day cool and pleasant, and horses doing well on the excellent feed. Latitude by observation of Camp 16, 23° 17' S. Night cool; thermometer at daylight, 50°. Distance, 15 miles.

Oct. 13.--Our course N.N.W. by compass, took us down the creek we had camped on, until it joined another water in several places. We crossed this creek, and at the end of 7½ miles from our camp we crossed a creek full of water, with an ana-branch flowing to the south-west. This I take to be the Alice. Hitherto we have been on fine downs all day; within half a mile farther we crossed a tributary coming from the north, and then another tributary. By keeping our course N.N.W. we again crossed the first creek, and camped on a fine reach of water. In the first tributary we saw the finest reach of water I have seen this side of the range, and at it was more than one black's camp. About 1 mile lower down than where we crossed the Alice, was a range on the right bank, which I named Mount Rodney, after one of my Murray men. As all three creeks meet there, I expect there must be a large quantity of water at the foot of it. The two tributaries both flow through acacia (gurrt) scrub for the last 5 miles; but where we have camped the country is more open, with promise of improvement. It will be observed that we have seen very little permanent water; but by following down the water-courses into the valley which lay to our right the last two days, I would expect to find abundance. Distance (direct) 11 miles.

Oct. 14.--The country at first was more thickly covered with acacia than suited me; and as we now had hit the creek again, I crossed it, and travelled parallel to it for a short distance 60° W. of N. by compass. The country now opened, and I resumed my N.N.W. compass course, which in about an hour and a quarter brought us to the summit of the downs ridge which separates the watershed of the Alice from that of the Thomson. Some low ranges were seen to the east, about 5 or 6 miles off, and a small one on the downs to the west, about 3 miles, is probably where the two creeks we have left take their rise. We now made 10 miles more over the downs, and as we descended stony plains came to a beautiful river, running W. by N. This, which is no doubt a tributary of the Thomson, I have called the Coreenda. Mr. Gregory, when he left the Thomson, says that river is formed by the small watercourses emanating from the sandstone ridges; had I thought that, I would not have ventured where I am now. This is splendid sheep country. I have no doubt that many of the holes in the Coreenda are permanent; but it is not possible to tell which, as that river has not long since ceased running. It floods occasionally about a quarter of a mile on each side, except where the downs approach the bank. The gum-trees look as if drought were a complete stranger to them, so fresh and healthy-looking are they. Distance, 14 miles.

Oct. 15. At Camp 18.--This day was one of disappointment, for the boy Jemmy Cargara returned in the afternoon without three of the horses, which he had been seeking since daylight. This is the first time he has failed. I now sent out three men on horseback, and they returned with the horses at three. Shortly after I had unsaddled the remainder, Coreen Jemmy and Patrick reported having seen the tracks of a considerable number of horses. I sent a party to examine them; they returned and reported there was no doubt of the tracks; that they were very old, and had been there near a fine lagoon, about 2 miles above my camp, and in wet weather. Aneroid, 29.5.

Oct. 16.--The early part of to-day's journey was over plains covered with gurrt, at times rather too close; thence past a watercourse and two lagoons, to sandstone ridges, with needle-

46

grass--very uncomfortable travelling. Four miles from the lagoons we crossed the well-marked tracks of a very large party going a little N. of W. These tracks were very old, and had been made in wet weather. They will be visible probably for years to come, whereas mine, made in dry weather, will be obliterated the first rainy season. We then came on to the opposite declivity of the sandstone ridges, and from thence saw a high peak which I have called Mount Macalister, being 5° N. of W. by compass; and another bluff mount, which I have called Mount Horsefeldt. I now perceived why Leichhardt's tracks had been going west. He probably camped on the Coreenda, above where my men saw the horse-tracks; thence travelled parallel to my course, and, being higher up the ridges, saw the peak sooner than I did, and turned off towards it. I now saw I was getting too intimate with the dividing range, and altered my course to north-west by compass. One mile brought me to a small watercourse, with many small pools of temporary water, arid, as there was a sufficiency of good grass, I camped. How is it that the blacks here have iron tomahawks? One has evidently a broad axe. The blacks on the Nive, who are much nearer the settlements, have only stone tomahawks, some very fine ones. Distance, 25 miles.

Oct. 17.--Started early on a north-west course, when, having crossed a high ridge, we came on a river running to the S. of W. This I believe to be the principal head of the Thomson. Here were seen the old tracks of horses (Leichhardt's camp was probably lower down on this river). We proceeded on the same course, passing betwixt two basalt ridges. I now for a short distance diverged to W.N.W., to get on a plain, when I resumed the north-west course, over two basalt ridges. The basalt was injuring our horses' feet, and I turned again W.N.W. to get on the plains. We next crossed a creek followed by a ridge. I was now able to resume the north-west course, and we hit a nice lagoon, and another head of the Thomson running south-west betwixt these two, and going N.N.W. were again the well-defined tracks of Leichhardt's party (he must have had a considerable quantity of wet weather). He had, no doubt, from Macalister's Peak perceived he was on the verge of the desert, and turned again to his old N.N.W. course. I now turned 25° N. of W. to go to a peak rising off the downs. From this peak I saw displayed before me an awful waste of endless plains. My man Patrick, who ascended the peak with me, and who is accustomed to the immense plains of the Edward and Murrumbidgee, was struck with consternation, and he remarked to me, "There is no father side this country." Upon leaving this solitary peak, which I have called the Sentinel, I had to turn 10° W. of N. by compass. We passed betwixt two terminations of spurs, over one ridge, to a gumcreek, running by N. We searched in vain for water, and had to push on over the next ridge, reaching another creek with sufficient water for a day or two. Distance, 25½ miles.

Oct. 18. Spelled at Camp 20.--I took a ride for 3 miles down the creek, which runs W.N.W. through the plains. I found another long pool of water, but fast drying up. We went to the top of the next ridge to get a good view of the range. Found I must still keep 10° W. of N. by compass. I observed a high mountain in that direction, with a remarkable gap in it. I expect to cross Leichhardt's track again to-morrow: of course whether we see it will depend upon whether he was still travelling in a rain season or not. The ground dries up here very quick. The thermometer, from 12 to 2 P.M. was 96° in the shade; the aneroid is 29.4. By observations taken from two different stars this morning, our latitude is 21° 50', 20 miles more north than my dead reckoning, which previously never differed from the observations more than 3 miles. We have travelled over some very good downs since leaving the sandstone. Near the ranges the grass is sufficiently thick, but as they slope down to the plain it gets thinner and thinner.

Oct. 19.--Good travelling all day. We crossed some fine downs. At the end of the first 4 miles we crossed a creek running W.S.W., and shortly afterwards another running south-west; then came to a third which ran S.S.W.; 3 miles beyond, pulled up the last of the waters of the Thomson watershed. This one was running south. We were now rising fast, and we travelled 2 miles upon a plateau of downs. Seeing the gap I have spoken of a little on my right, I altered my course from 10° W. of N. by compass to north, and on the same plateau reached it. I now turned down the opposite fall 10° W. of N. by compass, and struck a large creek running in three and sometimes more channels. This creek runs W.N.W., and is evidently the beginning of a large river. Some very high mountains are now close to us to the north. The aneroid is now 29.2, or 23.19. The gap we have crossed could have been very little under the height of the main range: where we crossed it, the aneroid stood at 28.9. Distance, 21½ miles.

Oct. 20.--Thermometer at daylight, 66°. I steered N.N.W. by compass, over fine very high basaltic downs, but thinly grassed in some places; we passed a tributary of the creek or river we camped on last night, and camped on a much larger head of the same river, which I have called the Haughton. We unfortunately disturbed three blacks, and thus failed in having an interview. They left very much worn iron tomahawks in this camp, and I have added three new ones to it. The hole here, though of great size and depth, is nearly dry. There do not appear to have been any of the heavy rains here which fell on the Victoria, as well as on the coast, in July and August. There is no appearance of spring; the carrots, instead of being green, like what they were on the Alice waters, have for the last few days been quite brown and brittle. A very high mountain, E.N.E. from the camp (No. 22), I have named Mount Gilbee, after Dr. Gilbee, who moved the resolution that I should lead this party.

Oct. 21.--Started 30° W. of N., till we crossed a tributary of the Haughton; thence to the top of a scrubby spur of the range, on which Patrick shot a turkey. I had now to turn north by compass to get out on to a plain, then N. by W. by compass, and crossed another tributary of the Haughton. Here three of the men in vain looked for water, and we had to push on over a ridge for 2½ miles. I ran down a creek W.N.W. for 4 miles, and then W. by N. for 4 miles more, being enticed on from point to point by

49

the appearance of the gum-trees, and the hope of finding water to bring my mare on to it. I saw it was of no use, and turned to the top of a gap in a mountain I have called Pollux; another to the east I called Castor. I had now a fine view of the country to the north, and with my glass saw gum-trees across a plain about 5 miles off. We went down the slope of the downs, and reached some splendid reaches of water, evidently the back-water of a large river. We had, however, to leave four more horses on the downs, and it was dark before we got our saddles off. The horses, parched with thirst, having bad no water during a fearfully hot day, rushed into the water, packs and all; luckily no damage was done. Distance, 24½ miles.

Oct. 22.--A day's spell, as a matter of course, at Camp 23, Jingle, in collecting the horses to-day, saw the river, which he says is as big as the Dawson: we shall cross it to-morrow, and likewise another, which I think comes round a peak I saw from Mount Pollux, bearing by compass 12° E. of N. The downs here are well grassed, and if the climate is not too hot, this is as good sheep country as any in Australia. I have no doubt that permanent water is to be found near this, but that at our camp would not stand more than seven or eight months.

Oct. 23.--Went N.N.W. by compass, crossing the river, which is a sandy dry channel, 90 yards wide: this is an immense width, considering bow high we are, the aneroid standing at 29.15. In about an hour, on the same course, we crossed a large tributary, two-thirds of the width of the main river, which I have named the Barkly, after the Governor of Victoria. A short distance from this brought us to the tip of a basalt ridge; and as a range was now in our way, I turned 32° W. of N. to the top of another ridge, having crossed a small channel. I now turned 55° W. of N., and then due west to a small creek with two temporary water-holes and good grass. As I must cross the range, which I take to be a spur of the main range, I camped, not wishing to attempt more to-day. I hoped to cross Leichhardt's track, but we have seen no signs of it. As the Barkly is running north-west, I think it probable he followed it as long as it kept that course. I suppose this river, which I expect receives large tributaries from the north, is a principal feeder of Stuart's great lake, and that Eyre's Creek flows into it; if so, Burke must have struck it. The thermometer this morning at daylight was 64°; this evening at sundown 86°. The aneroid 29.15. Night squally, and aneroid rose to 29.25. Distance, 11½ miles.

Oct. 24.--When I got to the top of the range this morning, I found I was on an extensive basaltic tableland. The aneroid stood at 28.9. The range, with a peak which I saw from Mount Pollux, stood in the midst of this tableland. Two Very high mountains were seen about 18 miles off; one 10° E. of N., and the other 20° E. of N. The basalt was distressing to the horses, and we could not average 2 miles an hour. We were pulled up by a deep ravine with a large creek at the bottom, and lined with cliffs of basalt columns; and it was with some difficulty we found a slope of debris not too steep for our descent; and then great care had to be taken. On reaching the foot of the cliffs we ran down the creek W. by N. to a fine pool, where we camped, having been five hours doing (Distance) 6½ miles.

Oct. 25.--Made a fair start at 7.45 A.M. I followed down Jingle Creek, as I wished to clear the basaltic ranges if possible: 11½ miles in a general westerly direction, now brought us to the Barkly River, leaving which we ascended to a bit of downs. I now saw that a spur of the same basaltic ranges must make the Barkly run W.S.W.; and, as there was no help for it, I steered in that direction, crossing the river and camping at a fine pool of water, with good grass and open country--the 'beau ideal' of a camp. The large tributary which I have called the Macadam, must have joined the Barkly at the back of a spur I see from here, bearing 30° S. of E. I had a view of both of them from the tableland, and then a plain separated them. We have had lots of pigeons at this camp; a lagoon about half a mile from here is reported to be permanent; I shall probably see it to-morrow. The day has been very hot, and yet not oppressively so, owing to a breeze which, although blowing from the W.S.W., was, strange to say, cool. We have generally had cool breezes from the east hitherto, at night especially. After sundown the thermometer was 100°; aneroid, 29.2. Distance, 14½ miles.

Oct. 26.--I overtook the advance party, and found them in vain endeavouring to get a parley with some gins who were crouching in the long grass on the bank of the river. I gave them some tomahawks, which gave them more confidence. One old lady who spoke a language of which Jemmy Cargara understood a little, stated that she had seen men like me many years ago down the river; pointing W.S.W., she said another river joined it from the south-east; this must be the Haughton. She also, in pointing W.S.W., repeated the words "Caree Garee" several times. I now turned north-west by compass, but the basalt again made us turn S. by W. 10°, to a fine reach of water and fine feed for the horses. I determined to spell here a day before attempting the basalt, which, 'coute qui coute', I must surmount if I wish to get to the north. Jingle having seen a little black boy near this, Mr. Haughton went to the camp with three of my men, and where he fell in with three black men: they had with them one of the gins to whom I had given the tomahawks; this insured a friendly reception and them returned to my camp with Mr. Naughton. They gave us to understand by signs, and by as much of their language as Jemmy Cargara could comprehend, that this river flowed W.S.W. by compass into Careegaree; that it was joined by another large river from the north-east. If we went north-west by compass, after crossing that river, we would go over a range and then come to a river which ran north-west into Careegaree, by which we conclude they mean the Gulf of Carpentaria; the other must be Stuart's great lake. These blacks have superior spears, thrown by a womera. One of grass-tree jointed was of immense length; another, not quite so long, had three prongs, one of which was barbed with a bit of bone fastened on with gum. Thermometer 86° at sundown; at 12 to-day it was 88°, and 100° at 2 and 3 P.M. Aneroid 29.21. Distance, 13 miles.

Oct. 27.--Spelled (it being Sunday) at Camp 27. The thermometer at 1 A.M. was at 68°; the aneroid rose to 29.25, and subsequently to 29.32, but after 12 it went down to 29.19. Yesterday evening Mr. Haughton and I ascended the range, at foot of which is this camp. We found that it was still the same tableland of basalt we have been skirting: however, by rounding this point, we get, north-west, a short piece of good ground, and then must encounter the basalt again. Day very hot. Thermometer in shade 102° at 2 P.M.; 98° at 3; at sundown, 89°. The water at this camp no doubt stands a long time, but as at present it is only 5 feet deep, it cannot be deemed permanent, notwithstanding its great length. Jingle yesterday saw some large lagoons of permanent, or, as he terms it, old water, on the south side of the river; and as there is a chain of such lapons all along on that side under the downs, no doubt many are permanent: on this or the north side there are water-holes similar to that at this camp whenever the spurs of the basalt tableland approach the river. Jemmy Cargara, in looking for the horses this morning fell in with the blacks again, and among them was now an old man who spoke some words of his language. He said he doubted whether we should find water for the horses in the first river we had to cross. There is therefore more than one yet running into the Barkly across our course. He told Jemmy, that after crossing a river we should cross a range which came from Jemmy's country, meaning, of course, the main range. Lat. 20° 46'. 1½ diff. from dead reckoning.

Oct. 28.--Made an excellent 7 o'clock start. After rounding the spur at No. 27, we had 1½ hour's fair riding, north-west, until we reached the top of the basalt; then over this spur, the descent and a ravine in it being so broken as to cause me to fear some accident to the horses; luckily none took place, and 2½ hours' fast riding north-west, over good undulating downs, brought us to the first river, which I have called the Dutton, after my friend Mr. Charles B. Dutton. The old black's doubts as to the water proved correct, and as Rodney, by digging, found some within a few inches of the surface, I determined to camp and make a pool for the horses. To supply forty-eight horses was no light undertaking, but all hands worked with a will, and before sundown the horses were all satisfied, and had plenty to return to during the night. The small black ants here are such a nuisance that no one can sleep. Distance, 16 miles.

Oct. 29.--Pulled up very early at two nice pools of temporary water, with good grass, as I do not deem it prudent to pass water after the warning we have received. Distance 5 miles.

Oct. 30.--Went 30° W. of N. to a gap on a downs ridge; from thence saw a range ahead of us, and reached the summit in 7 miles, same course, having crossed two large creeks. We now travelled over this range, which was of red sandstone (of course clothed with spinifex grass), north-west, and this brought us to a fine channel of a river, where we disturbed a black digging for water. We ran this river, which I have called the Stawell, a short distance W. by N. by compass, where Rodney found a beautiful spring water-hole, where we camped. The feed for the horses is also excellent.[4] Thunder at night, and a few drops of rain. Distance, 14 miles.

---

[4] We had hardly unsaddled our horses, when the voices of blacks were heard. Jingle, Paddy, and Jemmy Cargara went down the river towards them, when, to their surprise, they were addressed in Yarrinaakoo, the language spoken by the blacks on the Comet, and told in angry terms to be off and not to come there. My men resented this treatment, but fearing my disapproval should they fire on them, as they wished to do, they came back and reported to me that these blacks were "coola." We now heard them shouting in all directions, very evidently collecting the others who were hunting. In the meanwhile we had our dinner. Shortly after they had collected what they deemed sufficient for their purpose, and we heard one party coming up the river, and another answering their calls from over the ridge near our camp. It was time now for us to be doing, so I directed Mr. Macalister, Mr. Haughton, Jingle, Paddy, and Coreen Jemmy to take steady horses and face the river mob, whilst Jack and Rodney, and Jemmy Cargara stopped with me to protect the camp and meet the hill party. The mounted party met about thirty men, painted and loaded with arms, and they charged them at once. Now was shown the benefit of breech-loaders, for such a continued steady fire was kept up by this small party that the enemy never was able to throw one of their formidable spears. Twelve men were killed, and few if any escaped unwounded. The hill mob

Oct. 31.--The question now was, what water were we on, and had we crossed the main range or not? The river below our camp turned a little S. of W. We went 11½ miles west by compass, over very good downs, with a skirt of scrub on our right, and the river trees visible a long way on our left. I now turned. W.S.W. by compass, for the sake of getting water, and came upon, not the Stawell, but a river coming from the north-east. Thunder at night, and a little rain. Distance (direct) 16½ miles.

---

probably got alarmed at the sound of the heavy firing, and did not consider it convenient to come to the scratch. The gins and children bad been left camped on the river, and, as there was no water there, our possession cf the spring was no doubt the 'casus belli'. They might have shared it with us had they chosen to do so. This unavoidable skirmish ensured us a safe night, otherwise I think there would have been some casualty in my party before morning, as they can throw their spears 150 yards.

November, 1861

November 1.--Spelled at Camp 31. The grass is very good here, and as we have now abundance of water we spell here to-day; to-morrow we must make another try for the main range. Yesterday evening I hit the Stawell below the junction of this, which my men have called the Woolgar River. The Stawell now runs south-west, and is evidently a large contributor to the Barkly. There must, I think, be water somewhere near this, for we saw three ducks pass in the night, and the cockatoos are numerous. The bed of the Woolgar River I measured, 111 yards from the foot of one bank to the other.

Nov. 2.--Spelled.

Nov. 3.--Spelled. At 3 P.M. thermometer 97°. Spring found down the river, latitude 20° 16'. Cool night.

Nov. 4.--Still at Camp 31. Men all day in vain searching for tracks of lost mare. Saw large pools of permanent water in the Stawell.

Nov. 5.--Started,an advance party N.N.W., and did not get away in pursuit of it till afternoon, and so missed it. It was dusk when we reached a tributary of the Stawell; Mr. Haughton had not, however, stopped here, and, as we could no more see the tracks, we searched for a spot to dig for water, as he had all the water-bags with him. The place we tried gave every symptom, but nothing beyond mud. There was no help for it, so having tied up the horses we tried to sleep. The night was quite cold. Distance (out camp), 18 miles.

Nov. 6.--Reached Camp 32, and stopped remainder of day. Mr. Haughton had got water in another tributary by digging. Some blacks had been encountered near the camp, who had attacked Paddy and Rodney, who were looking for water; one was killed by a shot from Paddy. Thermometer 104° in the shade at 3 P.M., but a cool breeze from south-west. Distance (from Camp 31), 26 miles.

Nov. 7.--Went N.N.W. by compass, over a tableland of red sandstone, after having crossed some downs near Patience Creek. I observed that rain had fallen not long ago, and the grass was green; but it made me feel very grateful when I found a small creek with abundance of good water, and fine feed for the horses. Barometer 29.11. Distance, 11 miles.

Nov. 8.--Notwithstanding the great heat, we managed to do 16 miles N.N.W. and 3 W. by N. down a creek, but no water. At first we tried to dig where we camped, but as the water came too slow, went half a mile further down, and there found a spring, which, being dug out, made a capital water-hole. Very good burnt grass here. Is this not a tributary of the Flinders? Ground very heavy all day. Aneroid 29.25. Distance, 19 miles.

Nov. 9.--So great was the heat and so heavy the ground, that the horses were much distressed, and it was a great comfort to find some bulrushes, good springs of water, and grass, at the end of 10 miles. Our course has been, on an average, 32° N. of W., and we had crossed over to a large creek still running W.N.W.

Nov. 10.--Great delay in collecting the horses, and did not start until 10; the consequence was, that the heat and heavy ground, the latter worse than ever, nearly brought us to a standstill. My course for first 2½ hours was N.W. by compass. I then turned 32° N. of W., when I reached a large river, with a fine pool of water 6 feet in depth. Short as the day's stage was, we were obliged to camp. (No. 36.) Distance, 10½ miles.

Nov. 11--Started early down the river, and reached another fine pool 14 feet deep, before the heat of the day. The ground is also harder. An anabranch turned me N.W. by compass, and hit the river again about 9 miles beyond. If the ground opens, instead of being the brushy sandy country we have encountered hitherto on these waters, I intend taking advantage of the moonlight nights. Distance, 24 miles.

Nov. 12.--Ground dreadfully heavy all day. This day, I find from Mr. Haughton's report, as well as my own experience, has knocked our horses out of time altogether, so I must spell here a couple of days. Distance, 15 miles.

Nov. 13.--Spelled. The thermometer at 109° at 5 P.M. in the shade; aneroid as high as 29.51.

Nov. 14.--Spelled. Upon looking at the horses, no one would suppose they were so completely done up, for none are in bad condition; but the dreadfully heavy ground, with the heat, brings them to a stand-still at the end of 8 miles. This is a melancholy, good-for-nothing country. Aneroid, 29.50. What does this mean; for the sky is very clear, and there is a cool breeze? The nights are still delightfully cool. There are flocks of bronze-winged pigeons at this hole. Thermometer at 3 P.M., 103° in shade; at sundown, 91°; Friday morning at daybreak, 61°.

Nov. 15.--We started at 5.30 P.M., and had a pleasant ride at first over hard ground W. by S. 10°, and then W.N.W.; this brought me to a pool of water, and I camped, for although we have a splendid moon the brush is too thick to travel by night. Distance, 7 miles.

Nov. 16.--To-day reached what I supposed to be the real river, the last two camps having been, as I suspected, on an ana-branch. The river turned us 32° N. of W. by compass; then a course of W.S.W. brought us to a pool where it was deemed prudent to camp. Aneroid, 29.64; thermometer at 2 P.M., 105° in shade. Distance, 8 miles.

Nov. 17.---To-day has been more encouraging; we got an early start, and passed W. by N. over ground which was rapidly improving and getting more sound. I now turned W. by S., and was delighted to see some box-trees. The ground now is quite hard along what I take to be an anabranch; this turned us W.N.W. first, and then 6° S. of W., till the watercourse was no longer visible; still keeping the same course we crossed over to another branch. This is still too small for the main river, but my men are inclined to think it is so notwithstanding. If so, this is not the Flinders, but merely a tributary; it now turned W.N.W. and then N.N.W., which brought us to a small pool of temporary water, at which we camped. As we had a gentle breeze blowing from the gulf, the day was not unpleasantly hot. At this camp (41) is a remarkable oval ring, planted all round with tall thin saplings placed about a foot apart; none of my men understand the meaning of it. Distance, 20 miles.

Nov. 18.--Managed to make camp before the heat of the day, when we found a pool of water, and as Jingle could find none within two or three miles lower, we camped. The morning was made pleasant by the cool breeze from north-west. The river to-day has averaged a course of 48° W. of N. by compass; it has a better defined channel, and we passed one lagoon only just dried up; after all it is a mere apology for a river. The ground still continues hard, and is nearly all closed with spinifex; Jingle saw large plains when looking for water lower clown; ther-mometer at 3 P.M., 104°; aneroid, 29.82. The pigeons, both at the last camp and at this, have been in large flocks; I was unwill-ing to expend powder, of which I have only three canisters left, but as I thought a change of diet beneficial, I allowed the men to shoot at this camp, and the result was we had twenty-seven pigeons. Distance, 12 miles.

Nov. 19.--Fell in to-day with some gins, who could give no information of white men, but gave us the pleasing intelligence that henceforth there was plenty of water. The country to-day is much more open, but there were no plains. Aneroid, 29:83; thermometer at 3 P.M., 103° in shade. The river is more respectable; it was joined by a creek from south-east 4 miles below Camp 42, where is an excellent pool with fish, and good burnt feed. Distance, 19½ miles.

Nov. 20.--For the first 6 miles travelled 30° W, of N. by compass; then N.N.W. for 2 miles, when we crossed the river, having to-day been on the right bank. It now for 1 mile kept the same course, N.N.W., and a plain extended along the south bank; but now it turned north by east for 3 miles, and then N.N.E. for 1 mile, when we came to a deep permanent water-hole, and five blacks with gins and children at it. A friendly intercourse was established, and I gave 'them some tomahawks. They were subsequently joined by ten or twelve more men. We camped here: the blacks on one side of the water, we on the other. As this north-east turn of the river was perplexing, an endeavour was made to ascertain which way it now went. The blacks made us understand clearly enough that this river now ran N.W. by N. by compass; we understood, but not so clearly, that it joined another running more to the westward. They told us to follow this watercourse, and we should at short intervals find plenty of holes like this one. Large plains lay to the north-west, and, strange to say, they used for this the word "coonical," the same as Weerageree and Coreen Jemmy's language. They said we must avoid going west, as the country was no good, like what we had seen if we came down this river. They had heard of no white fellows being to the N.W. or W.N.W. I now suspect that what Mr. Gregory called the eastern end of the Gilbert, is the real Flinders; and this I believe to be the tributary. The country is now good, but a large proportion is subject to inundation. It is a great relief to have done with the heavy sandy country--with spinifex and brush of melaleuca, and other rubbish. Aneroid, 29.85; thermometer, at 2.30, 108° in the shade. The north-west breeze was cool this morning, but after 12 it now and then brought a hot blast from off the plains, which are visible from the back of this camp (No. 44). Distance, 13 miles.

Nov. 21. I went the course directed by the blacks, N.W. by N., but as this brought me, after passing the flooded plains, to heavy sand, I turned off north, and found a chain of good water-holes in the river, with good grass, and there camped. My men got a few fish here, about half a pound weight each. Thermometer in shade, 108° at 3 P.M.; aneroid, 29.84. Distance, 9½ miles.

Nov. 22.--To-day I followed the course of the river, merely cutting off the bends. Great doubts are entertained as to what river this is, for if it is the Flinders, I am 20 miles out in my longitude, and the way the blacks point, it ought to take me by my map to the camp of 11th of September of Gregory; but how this can be is a puzzle, considering the width of the inundations and the abundance of permanent water. How does this correspond with Gregory's dry irregular channels? Camped at one of the finest sheets of water I have seen for many a day. Our latitude, both by observation and dead reckoning, is 18° 18', and this corresponds with Gregory's 11th September camp, and so does my longitude. Distance, 17 miles.

Nov. 23.--We went the first hour north-west, and then north of west brought us round the end of a magnificent reach of water to some small pools to camp. In the afternoon I rode out to reconnoitre. I saw the river was now going a little east of north, and was again in long reaches. I struck out to the west, and came on some box-flats, and on my return to camp passed a lagoon, which I had no doubt was that which Gregory passed on his way from 10th September camp to that of 11th September. My map is right after all, and this I suppose is the river marked on the maps as Bynoe. Distance uncertain.

Nov. 24.--I went out a little to the N. of W. by N., and camped on the creek on which Gregory camped 10th September. Distance, 5 miles.

Nov. 25.--This eventful day, on a course W. by S. 5°, by compass, brought us to the Flinders River. We found it a beautiful large river, with high banks, and a delicious cool breeze blowing up it. We got a good many ducks, which were very acceptable, for our meat was finished yesterday. At this camp, latitude 18° 7', were found the well-defined trail of either three or four camels, and one horse: they had come down the Flinders. This night we had a tremendous thunder-storm; the first heavy rain we have had since starting from Bauhinian Downs. Distance, 16 miles.

Nov. 26.--I had to go up the river 8 miles before I could get a crossing-place, and last night's rain had made the ground so heavy that the horses were much distressed. I therefore camped as soon as we had crossed. This morning Jemmy Cargara, in collecting the horses, found Burke's trail returning across the plain, and going S.S.E. Grateful Creek, at Camp 33, and the three large creeks crossed upon leaving it, are evidently the heads of the Flinders, but the southerly trend which the main one took caused me to cross it. The tableland is therefore the dividing range. Distance, 8½ miles.

Nov. 27.--We went west by compass, crossing Gregory's 8th September creek half-way. We have had plains all day, but I can see low sandstone ranges not far on our left. Night oppressive. Aneroid fell to 29.96 from 29.84. Distance, 18 miles.

Nov. 28.--Started W. by N. At first we passed over plains so full of holes as to be distressing to the horses, who were constantly stumbling. We now crossed a creek with deep holes, but now dry. Higher up, where I saw many calares and a clump of trees, I think there is water. We now began to rise, and crossed over a spur of red sandstone ranges. Crossed two dry channels, then a ridge of good downs, and finally reached one head of Morning Inlet, and camped on some lagoons. This is very good pastoral country, but I fear too hot for sheep. There is much thunder hanging about, and some storms appear to have again fallen on the Flinders, but none have reached us. A cool N N.W. breeze rendered the afternoon very pleasant, but the forenoon was very oppressive. The immense plains which stretch away to the north and north-west, I suppose are the same mentioned by Captain Stokes. Sent a rocket up at night. Distance, 15 miles.

Nov. 29.--Expected a storm, but it passed over. Reached the main head of Morning Inlet, on a course west by north. After rising from the creek at last camp, we rode over red sandstone all day until we descended to box-flats, near the main creek: the first part box-trees, broad-leaved and good grass; and the latter portion melaleuca, nearly no grass, and with innumerable cones, some 6 feet high, made by the ants. On the banks of Morning Inlet was again, where the sandstone abutted on the creek, the hateful spinifex grass. The plains are visible north of this camp (53). Cool breeze from north-west. Night very oppressive and sultry. Mosquitoes triumphant. Distance, 9 miles.

Nov. 30.--After having crossed, not far from camp, three creeks, or branches of a creek, we cleared the sandstone, and rode across a fine plain, with a small creek in the centre, and found on the west side a large creek, with two anabranches, and a fine lagoon. We now crossed a sandstone ridge, with good grass and box-trees, and reached a plain, on leaving which we had to pass over downs and stony plains, of an excellent description for pastoral purposes, to a hole in a good downs creek. I was very glad to water the horses. Another mile brought me to where Mr. Macalister had judiciously decided on camping on a creek evidently flowing into the Leichhardt, which cannot be much more than 2 miles ahead of us; indeed, I think I can see the trees of it. Distance, 17 miles.

December, 1861

December 1.--To-day has been an annoying day. I first
went W. by N. to some sandstone cliffs, descended from them
W.S.W. to a saltwater creek, which we had to run up E.S.E. for
nearly 4 miles, and the last corner took us east to complete the 4
miles, so that we have come back parallel to our course. We now
found some small holes of fresh water; having crossed this, we
went W. by N. and W.N.W., when we at last got to the Leichhardt River--the water as salt as brine. We ran it up S.S.E. by
compass for 8 miles, passed by a black fishing at what looked
like a ford, just above the junction with a creek, which I take to
be that of Gregory's camp, 3rd September. The black never saw
us. There was now a good crossing place, but as Jingle signal-
ized there was fresh water in a creek at the back of a plain close
at hand, I went to it and camped. My men shot two ducks in the
river, and a couple of blacks were watching them a little lower
down the river. After dinner, or a make-shift for one, my men
went over towards the river in hopes of getting some ducks; but
as they were crossing the plain they saw two mobs of blacks approaching. As their appearance looked hostile, they returned to
camp. Presently it was reported that they were stretching out in a
half moon, in three parties. This move, which my men term
"stockyarding," is peculiar to blacks throwing spears with a
woomera, the object being to concentrate a shower of spears. It
was one long familiar to me, and I charged their left wing. The
result was that the circular line doubled up, the blacks turned and
fled. Their right wing, which was the strongest, got over the

river and were off; but the centre and left wing suffered a heavy loss. Distance uncertain.

Dec. 2.--Rodney found in a black's camp a sailor's jumper and an empty cognac bottle. The men (black) have all gone to the river to shoot ducks, for I cannot cross over until low water, which will be about 2 P.M. After crossing I made for Gregory's Creek, of 3rd September, and there camped, reaching it in four hours. Distance not given.

Dec. 3.--Went W.N.W. to the Albert River; found plenty of grass and the water fresh, but with a suspicion of salt; more decided when the tide rose. We had crossed an alternate succession of plains and flooded, box-flats with small watercourses. Gun heard down the river at 8.7 P.M. Distance, 22 miles.[5]

Dec. 5.--Mr. Macalister had found Gregory's marked tree, and also a bottle under ground, near a tree, marked by Captain Norman, with directions to dig. The bottle contained a note, stating the depot of the Victoria was about 12 miles lower down on the left bank. We now having saddled up, went up the creek until we could cross it, just above where I had slept last night. We then went N.W. by W. to Beame's Brook. Some delay took place, owing to the creek being boggy, and I was glad to camp as soon as we had crossed, for I was unwell from yesterday's anxiety and fatigue; and as Captain Norman's note is dated 29th November, there is now good hope of our meeting to-morrow. [Distance uncertain.]

Dec. 6.--Proceeded E.N.E., but had to camp, in order to make all safe for a storm. Night dismal, but the sound of a can-

---

[5] It now appeared that Camp 57 was 8 miles only from Victoria Depot, but having started to reconnoitre with a single attendant, Mr. Walker fell in with hostile natives, from whom he narrowly escaped, and had to camp out. The second in command had meanwhile been ordered to camp higher up, as it was not known the night before that the depot was so near. Next morning, 5th December, they arrived safe at camp.—Ed.

non within two or three miles was a comfort, and produced loud cheers. Distance, 16 miles.

Dec. 7.--In 2 miles, through a pelting hurricane of rain, reached the depot, and I had the pleasure of shaking hands with Captain Norman.

FREDERICK WALKER,

Leader of the Expedition.[6]

---

[6] This paper completes the narrative of the various expeditions despatched in search of Messrs. Burke and Wills; Mr. Howitt's expedition, which rescued King, as published in Vol. XXXII. of the *Society's Journal*, p. 430, having for the most part traversed ground so well known as to render it unnecessary to reproduce it 'in extenso'.—Ed,

Also from Benediction Books ...
Wandering Between Two Worlds: Essays on Faith and Art
Anita Mathias
Benediction Books, 2007
152 pages
ISBN: 0955373700

Available from www.amazon.com, www.amazon.co.uk

In these wide-ranging lyrical essays, Anita Mathias writes, in lush, lovely prose, of her naughty Catholic childhood in Jamshedpur, India; her large, eccentric family in Mangalore, a sea-coast town converted by the Portuguese in the sixteenth century; her rebellion and atheism as a teenager in her Himalayan boarding school, run by German missionary nuns, St. Mary's Convent, Nainital; and her abrupt religious conversion after which she entered Mother Teresa's convent in Calcutta as a novice. Later rich, elegant essays explore the dualities of her life as a writer, mother, and Christian in the United States-- Domesticity and Art, Writing and Prayer, and the experience of being "an alien and stranger" as an immigrant in America, sensing the need for roots.

About the Author

Anita Mathias is the author of *Wandering Between Two Worlds: Essays on Faith and Art.* She has a B.A. and M.A. in English from Somerville College, Oxford University, and an M.A. in Creative Writing from the Ohio State University, USA. Anita won a National Endowment of the Arts fellowship in Creative Nonfiction in 1997. She lives in Oxford, England with her husband, Roy, and her daughters, Zoe and Irene.

Visit Anita's website
    http://www.anitamathias.com,
and Anita's blog
    http://dreamingbeneaththespires.blogspot.com, (Dreaming Beneath the Spires).

The Church That Had Too Much
Anita Mathias
Benediction Books, 2010
52 pages
ISBN: 9781849026567

Available from www.amazon.com, www.amazon.co.uk

The Church That Had Too Much was very well-intentioned. She
wanted to love God, she wanted to love people, but she was both
hampered by her muchness and the abundance of her posses-
sions, and beset by ambition, power struggles and snobbery.
Read about the surprising way The Church That Had Too Much
began to resolve her problems in this deceptively simple and en-
chanting fable.

About the Author

Anita Mathias is the author of *Wandering Between Two Worlds:
Essays on Faith and Art.* She has a B.A. and M.A. in English
from Somerville College, Oxford University, and an M.A. in
Creative Writing from the Ohio State University, USA. Anita
won a National Endowment of the Arts fellowship in Creative
Nonfiction in 1997. She lives in Oxford, England with her husband, Roy, and her daughters, Zoe and Irene.

Visit Anita's website
    http://www.anitamathias.com,
and Anita's blog
    http://dreamingbeneaththespires.blogspot.com (Dreaming Beneath the Spires).

www.ingramcontent.com/pod-product-compliance
Lightning Source LLC
Chambersburg PA
CBHW021219020426
42331CB00003B/383